By the Editors of Best Recipes

Best Recipes

PASTA

COOKBOOK

SMITHMARK

INTRODUCTION

The great-tasting recipes in BEST RECIPES PASTA were gathered from a variety of recipe contests and cook-offs across America. The best have been selected for this collection of delicious soups, tempting salads, marvelous casseroles and innovative sauces. Each recipe has its own mouth-watering photograph and lists the name of the winner and the contest they entered.

Louis Weber, C.E.O.
Publications International, Ltd.
7373 North Cicero Avenue
Lincolnwood, Illinois 60646

Permission is never granted for commercial purposes.

This edition published in 1991 by SMITHMARK Publishers Inc., 112 Madison Avenue, New York, NY 10016

SMITHMARK books are available for bulk purchase for sales promotion and premium use. For details write or telephone the Manager of Special Sales, SMITHMARK Publishers Inc., 112 Madison Avenue, New York, NY 10016. (212) 532-6600.

Photography by Sacco Productions Limited/Chicago.
Photographers: Catherine Money and Warren Hansen
Photo Stylist/Production: Paula Walters and Betty Karslake
Food Stylists: Donna Coates and Lois Hlavac

ISBN: 0-8317-0598-1

Library of Congress Catalog Card Number: 91-60346

Pictured on the front cover: Wisconsin Swiss Linguine Tart (*page 82*).

Pictured on the back cover, (*clockwise from top*): Spinach Stuffed Manicotti (*page 20*), An Early Spring Pasta (*page 78*), Quick Beef Soup (*page 80*) and Beef Oriental (*page 30*).

First published in the United States.

Manufactured in Yugoslavia.

8 7 6 5 4 3 2 1

By the Editors of Best Recipes

Best Recipes

PASTA

COOKBOOK

SUPERB SALADS   4

ENTICING ENTREES   18

LUSCIOUS LASAGNA   44

SAVORY SAUCES   56

PASTA POTPOURRI   80

INDEX   96

SUPERB SALADS

When pasta is served with legumes all the essential amino acids are present, making it a good choice for a vegetarian meal.

Seafood Pea-Ista Salad

♦ Kathy Lewis from Murchison, Texas was the second place winner at the Black-Eyed Pea Jamboree in Athens, Texas.

Makes 4 to 6 servings

½ cup mayonnaise or salad dressing
¼ cup zesty Italian salad dressing
2 tablespoons grated Parmesan cheese
2 cups canned green or yellow black-eyed peas, rinsed
8 ounces corkscrew pasta, cooked, rinsed and drained
1½ cups chopped imitation crabmeat (about 8 ounces)
1 cup broccoli flowerets, partially cooked
½ cup chopped green pepper
½ cup chopped tomato
¼ cup sliced green onions

Combine mayonnaise, Italian salad dressing and cheese in large bowl; blend well. Add peas, pasta, imitation crabmeat, broccoli, pepper, tomato and onions; toss gently to mix. Cover; refrigerate at least 2 hours.

Thai Chicken Fettuccine Salad

♦ Jackie Stephens from Nashville, Tennessee was the grand prize winner in the "Pick up the Pace®" recipe contest sponsored by Pace Foods, Inc.

Makes 4 servings

     1 cup PACE® picante sauce
    ¼ cup chunky peanut butter
     2 tablespoons honey
     2 tablespoons orange juice
     1 teaspoon soy sauce
    ½ teaspoon ground ginger
     6 ounces uncooked fettuccine, hot cooked and drained
     3 chicken breast halves (about 12 ounces), boned, skinned and cut into 1-inch pieces
     2 tablespoons vegetable oil
       Lettuce or savoy cabbage leaves (optional)
    ¼ cup coarsely chopped cilantro
    ¼ cup peanut halves
    ¼ cup thin red pepper strips, cut into halves
       Additional PACE® picante sauce (optional)

Combine picante sauce, peanut butter, honey, orange juice, soy sauce and ginger in small saucepan. Cook and stir over low heat until blended and smooth. Reserve ¼ cup picante sauce mixture. Place fettuccine in large bowl. Pour remaining picante sauce mixture over fettuccine; toss gently to coat.

Cook chicken in oil in large skillet over medium-high heat until browned and cooked, about 5 minutes. Add reserved picante sauce mixture; mix well. Arrange fettuccine over lettuce-lined platter. Top with chicken mixture. Sprinkle cilantro, peanut halves and pepper strips over top. Refrigerate to cool to room temperature. Serve with additional picante sauce. Garnish as desired.

Rainbow Pasta Salad

♦ Jodi Magrum from Braddock, North Dakota was the fourth place winner in the Sensational Salads Pasta Contest sponsored by the North Dakota Wheat Commission.

Makes 4 servings

8 ounces uncooked tricolor corkscrew pasta, cooked, rinsed, drained and cooled
2 cans (4½ ounces each) medium shrimp, drained *or* ½ pound cooked fresh shrimp, peeled
½ cup chopped walnuts (optional)
¼ cup French salad dressing
¼ cup mayonnaise
2 tablespoons sliced pimiento-stuffed green olives
1 teaspoon finely chopped onion
Lettuce leaves
Grape clusters (optional)
Lemon peel strips (optional)

Combine pasta, shrimp, walnuts, salad dressing, mayonnaise, olives and onion in large bowl; toss gently to coat. Cover; refrigerate at least 2 hours. Serve over lettuce. Garnish with grapes and lemon peel.

Ingredients are added to give pasta its color. Beets and tomatoes make a reddish color, carrots make an orange color, spinach makes a green color and squid ink makes a black color.

The artichoke, long considered a mysterious delicacy, is available all year. Artichokes have a subtle, sweet and somewhat nutty flavor. During spring months artichokes should be bright green. They may appear bronzed in winter. Don't worry, these artichokes are "winter-kissed" by frost, which doesn't affect flavor.

Pasta Salad in Artichoke Cups

♦ Richard Hansen was a finalist in the Castroville Artichoke Festival, Castroville, California.

Makes 6 servings

   5 cloves garlic
   ½ cup white wine
   6 medium artichokes for cups
   1 lemon, cut into halves
   1 tablespoon *plus* 1 teaspoon olive oil, divided
      Chicken broth
      Basil Vinaigrette Dressing (recipe follows)
   8 ounces uncooked corkscrew pasta or pasta twists, cooked, rinsed and drained
   ½ teaspoon dried basil leaves, crushed
   2 cups sliced cooked artichoke hearts (not marinated)

Simmer garlic and wine in small saucepan 10 minutes. Meanwhile, cut bottoms of artichokes flat and remove outer leaves. Cut 1 inch from tops; snip tips from remaining leaves and rub ends with lemon. Add artichokes, wine-garlic mixture and 1 tablespoon oil to 2 inches boiling chicken broth in large saucepan. Cover; simmer 25 to 30 minutes or until leaves pull easily from base. Drain.

Prepare Basil Vinaigrette Dressing. Sprinkle pasta with remaining 1 teaspoon oil and basil.

Combine pasta, sliced artichoke hearts and 1 cup dressing in large bowl; toss gently to coat. Carefully, spread outer leaves of whole artichokes; remove the small heart leaves and scoop out the fuzzy choke. Fill with pasta mixture. Cover; refrigerate until serving time. Serve with remaining dressing. Garnish as desired.

Basil Vinaigrette Dressing: Combined ⅓ cup wine vinegar, 2 tablespoons Dijon mustard and 3 minced garlic cloves in blender or food processor. Cover; pulse until garlic is well mixed. Add ¾ cup coarsely cut fresh basil leaves; pulse mixture to blend. With motor running, slowly pour in 1 cup olive oil. Add salt and pepper to taste.

Chicken Salad Deluxe

♦ Julie Billstein from Shoreville, Minnesota was a first place winner in the Sensational Salads Pasta Contest sponsored by the North Dakota Wheat Commission.

Makes 20 servings

1¼ cups prepared buttermilk salad dressing
½ cup mayonnaise
3 tablespoons half-and-half
1¾ teaspoons Beau Monde seasoning
1 teaspoon salt
½ teaspoon pepper
5 whole chicken breasts (about 2 pounds), skinned, cooked and cubed
10 ounces uncooked 100% semolina medium shell macaroni, cooked, rinsed, drained and cooled
3 cups diced celery
2½ cups seedless green grapes, cut lengthwise into halves
1 package (12 ounces) slivered almonds, reserve 1 tablespoon for garnish
2 cans (2.25 ounces each) sliced water chestnuts, drained
½ cup chopped onion
Lettuce leaves
Parsley (optional)
Sliced star fruit (optional)
Cantaloupe slices

Combine salad dressing, mayonnaise, half-and-half, seasoning, salt and pepper in small bowl; blend well. Cover; refrigerate overnight to blend flavors.

Combine chicken, shells, celery, grapes, almonds, water chestnuts and onion in large bowl. Pour dressing over salad; toss gently to coat. Serve on lettuce. Garnish with reserved almonds, parsley and star fruit. Serve with cantaloupe slices.

Rotini Salad

♦ Diane Amble from Sarles, North Dakota was the fifth place winner in the Sensational Salads Pasta Contest sponsored by the North Dakota Wheat Commission.

Makes 8 to 10 servings

  2 to 3 stalks broccoli
 10 ounces uncooked rotini, cooked, rinsed, drained and cooled
  1 can (6 ounces) small pitted ripe olives, drained
 10 to 12 cherry tomatoes, cut into halves
 ½ medium red onion, thinly sliced
 ½ cup Italian salad dressing
  1 to 2 tablespoons grated Parmesan cheese (optional)
    Freshly ground black pepper
    Carrot strips (optional)

Cut flowerets from broccoli. Peel stalks; cut into chunks. Cook broccoli in boiling salted water in medium saucepan over medium-high heat just until broccoli is bright green and tender-crisp. Drain; rinse under cold water and drain thoroughly. Combine broccoli, rotini, olives, tomatoes, onion and salad dressing in large bowl. Add cheese. Season to taste with pepper. Toss gently to coat. Cover; refrigerate at least 2 hours. Garnish with carrot strips.

Cleaning Squid

The edible parts of a squid are the tubular body sac, the tentacles and fins. To clean, carefully pull the head from the body sac; discard the transparent quill and viscera. Wash the inside of the body sac. Pull off and discard the purplish outer skin that covers the sac and fins. Pull off the fins and reserve. Cut the tentacles from the head; discard head. Remove and discard the hard beak from the tentacles.

Fresh Seafood and Linguine Salad

♦ Alex DeSantis, Sr. from East Windsor, New Jersey was a prize winner in the New Jersey's Fabulous Winning Shellfish Recipes sponsored by the Fisheries Promotion Program, New Jersey Department of Agriculture.

Makes 6 servings

1½ pounds small squid, cleaned
  4 pounds mussels, scrubbed and beards
      removed
1½ to 3 dozen clams, scrubbed
  8 ounces uncooked linguine, cooked, rinsed
      and drained
    Olive oil
  ¼ cup freshly squeezed lemon juice
  2 cloves garlic, minced
  ½ teaspoon salt
  ¼ teaspoon pepper
  1 red onion, thinly sliced and separated into
      rings (optional)
  ⅓ cup finely chopped Italian parsley (optional)

Rinse squid thoroughly. Cut bodies into ¼-inch rings; finely chop tentacles and fins. Steam mussels and clams until just open; do not remove from shells. Discard any unopened shells. Toss linguine with 2 tablespoons olive oil.

Add just enough olive oil to large saucepan to cover bottom. Heat over medium heat; add squid. Cook, stirring constantly, 2 minutes. Place squid in large glass bowl. Add linguine, mussels and clams.

Combine ½ cup olive oil, lemon juice, garlic, salt and pepper in small bowl; blend well. Pour over salad; toss gently to coat. Cover; refrigerate at least 3 hours. Adjust seasoning with additional lemon juice, salt and pepper, if necessary. Garnish with onion rings and parsley.

ENTICING ENTREES

Peeling Garlic Cloves

To quickly peel whole garlic cloves, place the desired number of cloves in a small glass custard cup. Microwave at HIGH (100% power) until slightly softened, 5 to 10 seconds for 1 clove or 45 to 55 seconds for a whole head. Then just slip the garlic out of its skin; nothing could be easier! For information on peeling cloves by a range-top method, see page 88.

Sweet Garlic with Chicken Pasta

♦ Chefs Suvit and Gordon from Washington, D.C. were semifinalists in the "Use Your Noodle" contest sponsored by the National Pasta Association.

Makes 6 to 8 servings

  8 ounces garlic, minced
5½ tablespoons olive oil
1½ pounds shiitake mushrooms, sliced
  2 cups fresh plum tomatoes, diced
  1 cup chopped green onions
  1 teaspoon crushed red pepper
  2 cups chicken broth
1½ pounds chicken breasts, grilled, skinned, boned and diced
  1 package (16 ounces) uncooked bow tie noodles, cooked, rinsed and drained
  4 ounces cilantro, chopped and divided

Cook and stir garlic in hot oil in large skillet over medium-high heat until lightly browned. Add mushrooms, tomatoes, green onions and crushed red pepper. Cook and stir 2 minutes more. Add broth; simmer mixture to reduce slightly. Add chicken, noodles and ½ of the cilantro; heat through. Garnish with remaining cilantro.

Pasta that is "al dente" is tender but firm. Overcooked pasta is soft and shapeless.

Spinach Stuffed Manicotti

♦ Chef Toni Piccinini from San Francisco, California was a semifinalist in the "Use Your Noodle" recipe contest sponsored by the National Pasta Association.

Makes 4 servings

    1 teaspoon dried rosemary leaves, crushed
    1 teaspoon dried sage leaves, crushed
    1 teaspoon dried oregano leaves, crushed
    1 teaspoon dried thyme leaves, crushed
    1 teaspoon chopped garlic
 1½ teaspoons olive oil
 1½ cups canned or fresh tomatoes, chopped
    1 package (10 ounces) frozen spinach, cooked, drained and squeezed dry
    4 ounces ricotta cheese
    1 slice whole wheat bread, torn into coarse crumbs
    2 egg whites, lightly beaten
    8 uncooked manicotti shells, cooked, rinsed and drained
      Yellow pepper rings (optional)
      Sage sprig (optional)

Cook and stir rosemary, sage, oregano, thyme and garlic in oil in small saucepan over medium heat about 1 minute; do not let herbs turn brown. Add tomatoes; reduce heat to low. Simmer 10 minutes, stirring occasionally.

Combine spinach, cheese and bread crumbs in medium bowl. Fold in egg whites. Stuff manicotti with spinach mixture. Place ⅓ of the tomato mixture on bottom of 13×9-inch pan. Arrange manicotti in pan. Pour remaining tomato mixture over manicotti. Cover with foil. Bake in preheated 350°F. oven 30 minutes or until bubbly. Garnish with yellow pepper rings and sage sprig.

Tacos in Pasta Shells

♦ Mary Anne Alexander from Charlotte, North Carolina was third place winner in the Dairylicious Pasta Dishes contest sponsored by the Southeast United Dairy Industry Association, Inc., Atlanta, Georgia.

Makes 4 to 6 servings

1¼ pounds ground beef
  1 package (3 ounces) cream cheese with chives, cubed and softened
  1 teaspoon salt
  1 teaspoon chili powder
 18 uncooked jumbo pasta shells, cooked, rinsed and drained
  2 tablespoons butter, melted
  1 cup prepared taco sauce
  1 cup (4 ounces) shredded Cheddar cheese
  1 cup (4 ounces) shredded Monterey Jack cheese
1½ cups crushed tortilla chips
  1 cup dairy sour cream
  3 green onions, chopped
    Leaf lettuce (optional)
    Small pitted ripe olives (optional)
    Cherry tomatoes (optional)

Cook beef in large skillet over medium-high heat until brown, stirring to separate meat; drain fat. Reduce heat to medium-low. Add cream cheese, salt and chili powder; simmer 5 minutes.

Toss shells with butter; fill with beef mixture. Arrange shells in buttered 13×9-inch pan. Pour taco sauce over each shell. Cover with foil. Bake in preheated 350°F. oven 15 minutes. Uncover; top with Cheddar cheese, Monterey Jack cheese and chips. Bake 15 minutes more or until bubbly. Top with sour cream and onions. Garnish with lettuce, olives and tomatoes.

Saucy Mediterranean Frittata

♦ Charlotte Altenbernd from Lawrence, Kansas was third place winner in The Fifth Annual Kansas Egg Recipe Contest sponsored by the Kansas Poultry Association, Kansas State Board of Agriculture and American Egg Board.

Makes 4 to 6 servings

SAUCE
  1 can (8 ounces) tomato sauce
  1 teaspoon minced dried onion
  ¼ teaspoon dried basil leaves, crushed
  ¼ teaspoon dried oregano leaves, crushed
  ⅛ teaspoon minced dried garlic
  ⅛ teaspoon pepper

FRITTATA
  ⅓ cup chopped onion
  1 tablespoon olive oil
  1 medium tomato, chopped
  1 tablespoon finely chopped fresh basil *or*
      1 teaspoon dried basil leaves, crushed
  ¼ teaspoon dried oregano leaves, crushed
  ⅓ cup cooked orzo
  ⅓ cup chopped pitted ripe olives
  8 eggs
  ½ teaspoon salt
  ⅛ teaspoon pepper
  2 tablespoons butter
  ½ cup (2 ounces) shredded mozzarella cheese

For sauce, combine all sauce ingredients in small saucepan. Simmer over medium-low heat 5 minutes, stirring often. Set aside; keep warm.

For frittata, cook and stir onion in hot oil in *ovenproof* 10-inch skillet until tender. Add tomato, basil and oregano; cook and stir 3 minutes. Stir in orzo and olives; set aside. Beat eggs, salt and pepper in medium bowl. Stir in tomato mixture; set aside. Melt butter in same skillet. Add egg mixture; sprinkle with cheese. Cook over low heat 8 to 10 minutes or until bottom and most of middle is set. Broil 1 to 2 minutes or until top is browned. Serve with sauce. Garnish as desired. Cut into wedges to serve.

Spaghetti Rolls

♦ Christine Fried from Mandan, North Dakota was a prize winner in the Beef Cook-Off contest sponsored by the North Dakota CattleWomen and the North Dakota Beef Commission.

Makes 4 servings

1½ pounds ground beef
 1 tablespoon vegetable oil
 1 tablespoon onion powder
 1 teaspoon salt
 ½ teaspoon pepper
 2 cups spaghetti sauce, divided
 1 cup (4 ounces) shredded pizza-flavored cheese blend or mozzarella cheese
 1 package (8 ounces) uncooked manicotti shells, cooked, rinsed and drained

Cook beef in oil in large skillet over medium-high heat until brown, stirring to separate meat; drain fat. Stir in onion powder, salt and pepper. Stir in 1 cup of the spaghetti sauce; cool and set aside.

Reserve ½ cup of the ground beef mixture. Combine remaining beef mixture with cheese in large bowl. Stuff into manicotti. Arrange in greased 13×9-inch pan. Combine remaining spaghetti sauce with reserved beef mixture in small bowl; blend well. Pour over manicotti. Cover with foil. Bake in preheated 350°F. oven 20 to 30 minutes or until hot. Garnish as desired.

Oregano grows in profusion in the Mediterranean, spilling down the hillsides and filling the air with fragrance. Literally translated, it means "joy of the mountain."

Shrimp in Angel Hair Pasta Casserole

♦ William Sarnecky from Chester, Virginia was a first place winner in the Dairylicious Pasta Dishes contest sponsored by the Southeast United Dairy Industry Association, Inc., Atlanta, Georgia.

Makes 6 servings

1 tablespoon butter
2 eggs
1 cup half-and-half
1 cup plain yogurt
½ cup (4 ounces) shredded Swiss cheese
⅓ cup crumbled feta cheese
⅓ cup chopped parsley
¼ cup chopped fresh basil *or* 1 teaspoon dried basil leaves, crushed
1 teaspoon dried oregano leaves, crushed
1 package (9 ounces) uncooked fresh angel hair pasta
1 jar (16 ounces) mild, thick and chunky salsa
1 pound medium shrimp, peeled and deveined
½ cup (4 ounces) shredded Monterey Jack cheese
Snow peas (optional)
Plum tomatoes stuffed with cottage cheese (optional)

With 1 tablespoon butter, grease 12×8-inch pan. Combine eggs, half-and-half, yogurt, Swiss cheese, feta cheese, parsley, basil and oregano in medium bowl; mix well. Spread ½ of the pasta on bottom of prepared pan. Cover with salsa. Add ½ of the shrimp. Cover with remaining pasta. Spread egg mixture over pasta and top with remaining shrimp. Sprinkle Monterey Jack cheese over top. Bake in preheated 350°F. oven 30 minutes or until bubbly. Let stand 10 minutes. Garnish with snow peas and stuffed plum tomatoes.

$\mathcal{I}t$ is said that in Sicily, the housewives used to roll freshly made pasta onto knitting needles to dry, creating spiral shapes.

Beef Oriental

♦ Coreen Hoffert was a prize winner in the Beef Bash contest sponsored by the North Dakota CattleWomen and the North Dakota Beef Commission.

Makes 4 servings

- 1 pound ground beef
- 7 green onions, diagonally sliced into 2-inch pieces
- 3 tablespoons soy sauce
- ¼ teaspoon ground ginger
- 2 to 3 ribs celery, diagonally sliced into 1-inch pieces
- 8 mushrooms, sliced
- 1 package (20 ounces) frozen pea pods, rinsed under hot water and drained
- 1 can (8 ounces) tomato sauce
- 3 cups uncooked corkscrew pasta, cooked and drained
- 3 fresh tomatoes, cut into wedges
- 1 cup (4 ounces) shredded Cheddar cheese, divided
- 1 green pepper, cut into thin slices

Cook beef, onions, soy sauce and ginger in wok over medium-high heat until meat is brown, stirring to separate meat. Push mixture up the side of the wok. Add celery and mushrooms; stir-fry 2 minutes. Push up the side. Add pea pods and tomato sauce; cook 4 to 5 minutes, stirring every minute. Add pasta, tomatoes and ¾ cup of the cheese. Stir gently to combine all ingredients. Cook 1 minute. Add green pepper; sprinkle remaining cheese over top. Reduce heat to low; cook until heated through.

Sunday Super Stuffed Shells

♦ Paul and Ernie Filice from Gilroy, California were finalists in the Great Garlic Recipe Contest, sponsored by the Fresh Garlic Association and the Gilroy Garlic Festival, Gilroy, California.

Makes 9 to 12 servings

 3 cloves fresh garlic
 2 tablespoons olive oil
 ¾ pound ground veal
 ¾ pound ground pork
 1 package (10 ounces) frozen chopped spinach, cooked, drained and squeezed dry
 1 cup parsley, finely chopped
 1 cup bread crumbs
 2 eggs, beaten
 3 cloves fresh garlic, minced
 3 tablespoons grated Parmesan cheese
 Salt to taste
 1 package (12 ounces) uncooked jumbo pasta shells, cooked, rinsed and drained
 3 cups spaghetti sauce
 Sauteed zucchini slices (optional)

Cook and stir the 3 whole garlic cloves in hot oil in large skillet over medium heat until garlic is brown. Discard garlic. Add veal and pork; cook until lightly brown, stirring to separate meat; drain fat. Set aside.

Combine spinach, parsley, bread crumbs, eggs, minced garlic and cheese in large bowl; blend well. Season to taste with salt. Add cooled, meat mixture; blend well. Fill shells with stuffing.

Spread about 1 cup of the spaghetti sauce over bottom of greased 12×8-inch pan. Arrange shells in pan. Pour remaining sauce over shells. Cover with foil. Bake in preheated 375°F. oven 35 to 45 minutes or until bubbly. Serve with zucchini. Garnish as desired.

Noodles originated in Germany in the 13th century. Noodles derive their name from the German word "Nudeln" that means a pasta product made with eggs and shaped in ribbons.

Shrimp Noodle Supreme

♦ Glenda Beecher from Wray, Georgia was a finalist in the Dairylicious Pasta Dishes contest sponsored by the Southeast United Dairy Industry Association, Inc., Atlanta, Georgia.

Makes 6 servings

    1 package (8 ounces) uncooked spinach
        noodles, hot cooked and drained
    1 package (3 ounces) cream cheese, cubed and
        softened
 1½ pounds medium shrimp, peeled and
        deveined
    ½ cup butter, softened
      Salt and pepper to taste
    1 can (10¾ ounces) condensed cream of
        mushroom soup
    1 cup dairy sour cream
    ½ cup half-and-half
    ½ cup mayonnaise
    1 tablespoon chopped chives
    1 tablespoon chopped parsley
    ½ teaspoon Dijon mustard
    ¾ cup (6 ounces) shredded sharp Cheddar
        cheese
      Tomato wedges (optional)
      Parsley sprigs (optional)
      Lemon slices (optional)
      Paprika (optional)

Combine noodles and cream cheese in medium bowl. Spread noodle mixture in bottom of greased 13×9-inch glass casserole. Cook shrimp in butter in large skillet over medium-high heat until pink and tender, about 5 minutes. Season to taste with salt and pepper. Spread shrimp over noodles.

Combine soup, sour cream, half-and-half, mayonnaise, chives, chopped parsley and mustard in another medium bowl. Spread over shrimp. Sprinkle Cheddar cheese over top. Bake in preheated 325°F. oven 25 minutes or until hot and cheese melts. Garnish with tomato, parsley sprigs, lemon slices and paprika.

String Pie

♦ Melanie Cunningham was a prize winner in the Beef Bash contest sponsored by the North Dakota CattleWomen and the North Dakota Beef Commission.

Makes 6 to 8 servings

    1 pound ground beef
    ½ cup chopped onion
    ¼ cup chopped green pepper
    1 jar (15½ ounces) spaghetti sauce
    8 ounces spaghetti, hot cooked and drained
    ⅓ cup grated Parmesan cheese
    2 eggs, beaten
    2 teaspoons butter
    1 cup cottage cheese
    ½ cup (2 ounces) shredded mozzarella cheese

Cook beef, onion and green pepper in large skillet over medium-high heat until meat is brown, stirring to separate meat. Drain fat. Stir in spaghetti sauce; mix well. Combine spaghetti, Parmesan cheese, eggs and butter in large bowl; mix well. Place in bottom of 13×9-inch pan. Spread cottage cheese over top. Pour sauce mixture over cottage cheese. Sprinkle mozzarella cheese over top. Bake in preheated 350°F. oven until cheese melts, about 20 minutes.

Cheesy Chicken Roll-Ups

♦ Sheila Megill from Greenville, South Carolina was a finalist in the Dairylicious Pasta Dishes contest sponsored by the Southeast United Dairy Industry Association, Inc., Atlanta, Georgia.

Makes 6 servings

1 medium onion, diced
4 ounces fresh mushrooms, sliced
¼ cup butter
3 chicken breast halves, skinned, boned and cut into bite-sized pieces
¾ cup dry white wine
½ teaspoon dried tarragon leaves, crushed
½ teaspoon salt
½ teaspoon pepper
6 uncooked lasagna noodles, cooked, drained and each cut lengthwise into halves
1 package (8 ounces) cream cheese, cubed and softened
½ cup heavy cream
½ cup dairy sour cream
1½ cups (6 ounces) shredded Swiss cheese, divided
1 cup (4 ounces) shredded Muenster cheese, divided
3 tablespoons toasted sliced almonds
  Chopped parsley (optional)

Cook and stir onion and mushrooms in melted butter in large skillet over medium-high heat until tender. Add chicken, wine, tarragon, salt and pepper; bring to a boil. Reduce heat to low; simmer 10 minutes.

Curl each lasagna noodle half into a circle; arrange in greased 13×9-inch pan. Using a slotted spoon, fill center of lasagna rings with chicken mixture. To remaining liquid in skillet, add cream cheese, heavy cream, sour cream, ¾ cup of the Swiss cheese and ½ cup of the Muenster cheese. Cook and stir until cheeses melt; do not boil. Pour over lasagna rings. Sprinkle remaining cheeses and almonds on top. Bake in preheated 325°F. oven 35 minutes or until bubbly. Sprinkle with parsley. Garnish as desired.

Polish Reuben Casserole

◆ Darlene Lutz from New England, North Dakota was third place winner in "Casseroles of the Century" Pasta Contest sponsored by the North Dakota Wheat Commission.

Makes 8 to 10 servings

- 2 cans (10¾ ounces each) condensed cream of mushroom soup
- 1⅓ cups milk
- ½ cup chopped onion
- 1 tablespoon prepared mustard
- 2 cans (16 ounces each) sauerkraut, rinsed and drained
- 1 package (8 ounces) uncooked medium-width noodles
- 1½ pounds Polish sausage, cut into ½-inch pieces
- 2 cups (8 ounces) shredded Swiss cheese
- ¾ cup whole wheat bread crumbs
- 2 tablespoons butter, melted

Combine soup, milk, onion and mustard in medium bowl; blend well. Spread sauerkraut in greased 13×9-inch pan. Top with uncooked noodles. Spoon soup mixture evenly over top. Top with sausage, then cheese. Combine crumbs and butter in small bowl; sprinkle over top. Cover pan tightly with foil. Bake in preheated 350°F. oven 1 hour or until noodles are tender. Garnish as desired.

Polish Sausage is also called kielbasa. It is garlicky flavored and consists mainly of seasoned pork, although beef and veal are often added. It is commonly sold in long links that are smoked and precooked, ready to heat and serve. The method for making kielbasa has remained virtually unchanged for more than five hundred years and sausage connoisseurs consider it perfection.

Rigatoni with Four Cheeses

♦ Nancy Lazara was a winner in the Supermarket Chef's Showcase sponsored by the Wisconsin Milk Marketing Board.

Makes 6 servings

3 cups milk
1 tablespoon chopped carrot
1 tablespoon chopped celery
1 tablespoon chopped onion
1 tablespoon parsley sprigs
½ bay leaf
¼ teaspoon black peppercorns
¼ teaspoon hot pepper sauce
   Dash ground nutmeg
¼ cup butter
¼ cup all-purpose flour
½ cup grated Wisconsin Parmesan cheese
¼ cup grated Wisconsin Romano cheese
12 ounces uncooked rigatoni, cooked and drained
1½ cups (6 ounces) shredded Wisconsin Cheddar cheese
1½ cups (6 ounces) shredded Wisconsin mozzarella cheese
¼ teaspoon chili powder

Combine milk, carrot, celery, onion, parsley, bay leaf, peppercorns, hot pepper sauce and nutmeg in medium saucepan. Bring to a boil. Reduce heat to low; simmer 10 minutes. Strain; reserve milk.

Melt butter in another medium saucepan over medium heat. Stir in flour. Gradually stir in reserved milk. Cook, stirring constantly, until thickened. Remove from heat. Add Parmesan and Romano cheeses, stirring until blended. Combine rigatoni and sauce in large bowl; toss gently to coat. Combine Cheddar and mozzarella cheeses in medium bowl. Place ½ of the pasta mixture in buttered 2-quart casserole. Sprinkle cheese mixture over top; place remaining pasta mixture on top. Sprinkle with chili powder. Bake in preheated 350°F. oven 25 minutes or until bubbly. Garnish as desired.

LUSCIOUS LASAGNA

Mozzarella is a soft white cheese that melts easily. In southern Italy, where it originated, it is made from the milk of buffaloes. In other parts of Italy and in North America, it is made from cows' milk.

Lazy Lasagna

♦ Mrs. B.J. Thompson from Devils Lake, North Dakota was a finalist in the North Dakota Dairy Cookoff sponsored by the North Dakota Dairy Promotion Commission.

Makes 8 to 10 servings

- 1 pound ground beef
- 1 jar (32 ounces) spaghetti sauce
- 1 pound cottage cheese
- 8 ounces dairy sour cream
- 8 uncooked lasagna noodles
- 3 packages (6 ounces each) sliced mozzarella cheese (12 slices)
- ½ cup grated Parmesan cheese
- 1 cup water

Cook beef in large skillet over medium-high heat until meat is brown, stirring to separate meat; drain fat. Add spaghetti sauce. Reduce heat to low. Heat through, stirring occasionally; set aside. Combine cottage cheese and sour cream in medium bowl; blend well.

Spoon 1½ cups of the meat sauce in bottom of 13×9-inch pan. Place ½ of the uncooked noodles over sauce, then ½ of the cheese mixture, 4 slices of the mozzarella, ½ of the remaining meat sauce and ¼ cup of the Parmesan cheese. Repeat layers starting with the noodles. Top with remaining 4 slices of mozzarella cheese. Pour water around the sides of the pan. Cover tightly with foil. Bake in preheated 350°F. oven 1 hour. Uncover; bake 20 minutes more or until bubbly. Let stand 15 to 20 minutes. Garnish as desired.

Seafood Lasagne

♦ Mary Debly from Union, New Jersey was a finalist in the "Fishing for Compliments Recipe Contest" sponsored by the New Jersey Department of Agriculture and Ronzoni Pasta.

Makes 8 to 10 servings

1 large onion, chopped
2 tablespoons butter or margarine
1½ cups cream-style cottage cheese
1 package (8 ounces) cream cheese, cubed and softened
2 teaspoons dried basil leaves, crushed
½ teaspoon salt
⅛ teaspoon pepper
1 egg, lightly beaten
2 cans (10¾ ounces each) cream of mushroom soup
⅓ cup milk
1 clove garlic, minced
½ cup dry white wine
½ pound bay scallops
½ pound flounder fillets, cubed
½ pound medium shrimp, peeled and deveined
1 package (16 ounces) Ronzoni® Curly Edge Lasagne, cooked, rinsed and drained
1 cup (4 ounces) shredded mozzarella cheese
2 tablespoons grated Parmesan cheese

Cook onion in hot butter in medium skillet over medium heat until tender, stirring frequently. Stir in cottage cheese, cream cheese, basil, salt and pepper; mix well. Stir in egg; set aside.

Combine soup, milk and garlic in large bowl until well blended. Stir in wine, scallops, flounder and shrimp.

Place a layer of overlapping noodles in greased 13×9-inch pan. Spread ½ of the cheese mixture over noodles. Place a layer of noodles over cheese mixture and top with ½ of the seafood mixture. Repeat layers. Sprinkle with mozzarella and Parmesan cheeses. Bake in preheated 350°F. oven 45 minutes or until bubbly. Let stand 10 minutes.

Lasagna Supreme

◆ Michelle Watson from Sapulpa, Oklahoma was a finalist in the A-OK Cook Off sponsored by various Oklahoma agricultural organizations, Oklahoma City, Oklahoma.

Makes 8 to 10 servings

½ pound ground Oklahoma beef
½ pound mild Italian sausage
½ cup chopped onion
2 cloves garlic, minced
1 can (16 ounces) tomatoes, undrained and
  cut up
1 can (6 ounces) tomato paste
2 teaspoons dried basil, crushed
1 teaspoon dried marjoram, crushed
1 can (4 ounces) sliced mushrooms, drained
2 eggs
1 pound cream-style cottage cheese
¾ cup grated Parmesan cheese, divided
2 tablespoons parsley flakes
½ teaspoon salt
½ teaspoon pepper
8 ounces uncooked lasagna noodles, cooked,
  rinsed and drained
2 cups (8 ounces) shredded Cheddar cheese
3 cups (12 ounces) shredded mozzarella cheese
  Mixed salad (optional)

Cook meats, onion and garlic in large skillet over medium-high heat until meat is brown, stirring to separate meat; drain fat. Add tomatoes with juice, tomato paste, basil and marjoram. Reduce heat to low. Cover; simmer 15 minutes, stirring often. Stir in mushrooms; set aside.

Beat eggs in large bowl; add cottage cheese, ½ cup of the Parmesan cheese, parsley, salt and pepper. Mix well. Place ½ of the noodles in bottom of greased 13×9-inch pan. Spread ½ of the cheese mixture over noodles, then ½ of the meat mixture and ½ of the Cheddar and mozzarella cheeses. Repeat layers. Sprinkle with remaining ¼ cup Parmesan cheese. Bake in preheated 375°F. oven 40 to 45 minutes or until bubbly. Let stand 10 minutes. Serve with mixed salad.

Note: Lasagna may be assembled, covered and refrigerated. Bake in preheated oven 60 minutes or until bubbly.

Brooklyn, New York has the distinction of being the home to the first commercial pasta plant in the United States. It was founded in 1848.

Luscious Vegetarian Lasagna

♦ Ted Quanrud from Bismarck, North Dakota was a finalist in the North Dakota Dairy Cookoff sponsored by the North Dakota Dairy Promotion Commission.

Makes 6 to 8 servings

    1 can (14½ ounces) tomatoes, undrained
    1 can (12 ounces) tomato sauce
    1 teaspoon dried oregano leaves, crushed
    1 teaspoon dried basil leaves, crushed
      Dash black pepper
    1 large onion, chopped
 1½ teaspoons minced garlic
    2 tablespoons olive oil
    2 small zucchini, chopped
    8 ounces mushrooms, sliced
    1 large carrot, chopped
    1 green pepper, chopped
    1 cup (4 ounces) shredded mozzarella cheese
    2 cups 1% milkfat cottage cheese
    1 cup grated Parmesan or Romano cheese
    8 ounces uncooked lasagna noodles, cooked,
      rinsed and drained
      Parsley sprigs (optional)

Simmer tomatoes with juice, tomato sauce, oregano, basil and black pepper in medium saucepan over low heat. Cook and stir onion and garlic in hot oil in large skillet over medium-high heat until onion is golden. Add zucchini, mushrooms, carrot and green pepper. Cook and stir until vegetables are tender, 5 to 10 minutes. Stir vegetables into tomato mixture; simmer 15 minutes. Combine mozzarella, cottage and Parmesan cheeses in large bowl; blend well.

Spoon about 1 cup sauce in bottom of 12×8-inch pan. Place a layer of noodles over sauce, then ½ of the cheese mixture and ½ of the remaining sauce. Repeat layers of noodles, cheese mixture and sauce. Bake in preheated 350°F. oven 30 to 45 minutes or until bubbly. Let stand 10 minutes. Garnish with parsley.

Substitution: Other vegetables may be added or substituted for the ones listed above.

Pasta is an excellent source of complex carbohydrates. It also contains six essential amino acids, three B-complex vitamins and iron.

Spetzque

♦ Carla Ziegler, Robbie Vetter, Rachel Thomas and Michelle Grossmann are prize winners in the Beef Bash contest sponsored by the North Dakota CattleWomen and the North Dakota Beef Commission.

Makes 6 servings

2 pounds ground beef
1 can (4½ ounces) chopped ripe olives, drained
1 can (4 ounces) mushroom stems and pieces, drained
1 small onion, chopped
1 jar (16 ounces) spaghetti sauce
Dash pepper
Dash dried oregano leaves, crushed
Dash Italian seasoning
9 uncooked lasagna noodles, cooked, rinsed and drained
1¼ cups frozen corn
1¼ cups frozen peas
2 cups (8 ounces) shredded mozzarella cheese

Cook beef in large skillet over medium-high heat until meat is brown, stirring to separate meat; drain fat. Add olives, mushrooms and onion. Cook, stirring occasionally, until vegetables are tender. Add spaghetti sauce, pepper, oregano and Italian seasoning. Heat through, stirring occasionally; set aside.

Place ⅓ of the noodles in bottom of greased 13×9-inch pan. Spread ½ of the beef mixture over noodles, then ½ of the corn and peas. Repeat layers ending with noodles. Bake in preheated 350°F. oven 25 minutes. Sprinkle with cheese; bake 5 minutes more or until bubbly. Let stand 10 minutes. Garnish as desired.

Apple Lasagna

♦ Rhonda Jordahl from Fargo, North Dakota was third place winner in the Delicious Desserts Pasta Contest sponsored by the North Dakota Wheat Commission.

Makes 12 to 15 servings

2 cups (8 ounces) shredded Cheddar cheese
1 cup ricotta cheese
1 egg, lightly beaten
¼ cup granulated sugar
1 teaspoon almond extract
2 cans (20 ounces each) apple pie filling
8 uncooked lasagna noodles, cooked, rinsed and drained
6 tablespoons all-purpose flour
6 tablespoons packed brown sugar
¼ cup quick-cooking oats
½ teaspoon ground cinnamon
Dash ground nutmeg
3 tablespoons margarine
1 cup dairy sour cream
⅓ cup packed brown sugar

Combine Cheddar cheese, ricotta cheese, egg, granulated sugar and almond extract in medium bowl; blend well. Spread 1 can apple pie filling over bottom of greased 13×9-inch pan. Layer ½ of the noodles over filling, then spread cheese mixture over noodles. Top with remaining noodles, then remaining can of apple pie filling.

Combine flour, 6 tablespoons brown sugar, oats, cinnamon and nutmeg in small bowl. Cut in margarine until crumbly. Sprinkle over apple pie filling. Bake in preheated 350°F. oven 45 minutes. Cool 15 minutes.

Meanwhile, prepare garnish by blending sour cream and ⅓ cup brown sugar in small bowl until smooth. Cover; refrigerate.

To serve, cut lasagna into squares and garnish with sour cream mixture.

SAVORY SAUCES

Fettuccine with Duckling and Roasted Red Peppers

♦ Sharyn Lane from Coral Springs, Florida was second place winner in the Concord National Duckling Cookoff sponsored by Concord Farms®, Concord, North Carolina.

Makes 4 main-dish or 8 appetizer servings

> 1 **Concord Farms® Duckling (4½ to 5½ pounds), thawed and quartered**
> **Garlic powder**
> **Onion salt**
> 2 **tablespoons butter or margarine, melted**
> 1½ **tablespoons all-purpose flour**
> 1¼ **cups heavy cream**
> 2 **tablespoons grated Parmesan cheese**
> 1 **pound uncooked fettuccine, hot cooked and drained**
> ½ **cup prepared roasted red peppers, drained**
> ¼ **cup chopped walnuts**
> ¼ **cup sliced pitted ripe olives**

Place duckling, skin side up, on rack in shallow pan. Sprinkle with garlic powder and onion salt. Cook in 350°F. oven about 1½ hours or until internal temperature registers 185°F. when tested with a meat thermometer. Cool; remove bones and skin. Cut duckling into bite-sized pieces; set aside.

Combine butter and flour in medium saucepan; blend well. Cook 1 minute over medium heat. Gradually stir in cream. Stir in cheese. Cook until sauce thickens, stirring constantly.

Place fettuccine in large bowl. Add duckling, peppers, walnuts and olives. Pour sauce over fettuccine; toss gently to coat. Garnish as desired.

A handy tip from the California Tomato Advisory Board: To hasten ripening, place an apple in a paper bag with an unripe tomato.

Fresh Tomato Pasta Andrew

♦ Dahlia Haas from Los Angeles, California was the first place winner in the California Fresh Market Tomato Advisory Board Contest, Los Angeles, California.

Makes 2 main-dish or 4 appetizer servings

1 pound fresh tomatoes, cut into wedges
1 cup packed fresh basil leaves
2 cloves garlic, chopped
2 tablespoons olive oil
8 ounces Camenzola cheese *or* 6 ounces ripe Brie plus 2 ounces Stilton cheese, each cut into small pieces
Salt and white pepper to taste
4 ounces uncooked angel hair pasta, vermicelli or other thin pasta, hot cooked and drained
Grated Parmesan cheese

Place tomatoes, basil, garlic and oil in covered food processor or blender; pulse on and off until ingredients are coarsely chopped, but not pureed. Combine tomato mixture and Camenzola cheese in large bowl. Season to taste with salt and white pepper. Add pasta; toss gently until cheese melts. Serve with Parmesan cheese. Garnish as desired.

Zucchini is the most popular summer squash. Distinguished by their edible skins and seeds, summer squash differ widely in skin color and shape. But the mild, delicate flavor found in all varieties makes them largely interchangeable in recipe use.

Vegetable Seafood Pasta

♦ Terry Morse Spitale from River Ridge, Louisiana was a finalist in the Fish and Seafood category in the "Cookbook and Recipe Contest" sponsored by *The Times-Picayune*, New Orleans, Louisiana.

Makes 6 servings

1 medium onion, chopped
4 green onions, chopped
3 tablespoons *each* butter and olive oil
3 carrots, cut into strips
1 zucchini, cut into strips
1 *each* small red and yellow pepper, cut into strips
3 ounces snow peas
⅓ cup sliced mushrooms
3 cloves garlic, minced
½ pound *each* scallops and shrimp, peeled and deveined
⅔ cup clam juice
⅓ cup vermouth
1 cup heavy cream
1 egg yolk, beaten
⅔ cup flaked crabmeat
2 tablespoons *each* lemon juice and chopped parsley
½ teaspoon seafood seasoning
Freshly ground black pepper to taste
1 package (8 ounces) uncooked linguine, hot cooked and drained

Cook and stir onions in hot butter and oil in large skillet over medium-high heat until soft. Add vegetables and garlic; reduce heat to low. Cover; simmer until vegetables are tender. Remove; set aside. Cover and cook scallops and shrimp in same skillet over medium-low heat until opaque. Remove; reserve liquid in pan. Add clam juice; bring to a boil. Add vermouth; cook over medium-high heat 3 minutes, stirring constantly. Reduce heat to low; add cream, stirring constantly. Stir some of the sauce into yolk; stir back into sauce. Cook until thickened.

Add vegetables, shrimp, scallops and crabmeat to sauce. Heat through. Add remaining ingredients except linguine. Pour over linguine in large bowl; toss gently to coat.

Leftover pasta can be frozen and reheated or microwaved. Refrigerated pasta can be freshened by rinsing with hot or cold water, depending on how you plan to use it.

Pasta Delight

♦ Chef Cherif Brahmi from Dallas, Texas was a semifinalist in the "Use Your Noodle" contest sponsored by the National Pasta Association.

Makes 4 to 6 servings

1 medium zucchini, sliced
1 tablespoon olive oil
2 tablespoons chopped shallots
2 cloves garlic, chopped
1 medium tomato, diced
2 tablespoons chopped fresh basil *or*
   ½ teaspoon dried basil, crushed
2 tablespoons grated Parmesan cheese
12 ounces uncooked penne pasta, hot cooked
   and drained

Cook and stir zucchini in hot oil in large skillet over medium-high heat. Reduce heat to medium. Add shallots and garlic; cook 1 minute. Add tomato; cook and stir 45 seconds. Add basil and cheese. Pour vegetable mixture over penne in large bowl; toss gently to mix.

Non-egg pastas contain no cholesterol. Noodles (pasta made with eggs) are low in cholesterol.

Fusilli Pizziaola

◆ Chef A.E. Woodward, Jr. from Houston, Texas was a semifinalist in the "Use Your Noodle" contest sponsored by the National Pasta Association.

Makes 6 to 8 servings

  8 ounces mushrooms, sliced
  1 large red pepper, diced
  1 large green pepper, diced
  1 large yellow pepper, diced
 10 green onions, chopped
  1 large onion, diced
  8 cloves garlic, coarsely chopped
  3 large shallots, chopped
  ½ cup chopped fresh basil *or* 2 teaspoons dried
      basil leaves, crushed
  2 tablespoons chopped fresh oregano *or*
      1 teaspoon dried oregano, crushed
      Dash crushed red pepper
  ¼ cup olive oil
  4 cups canned or fresh tomatoes, chopped
      Salt and pepper to taste
  1 package (16 ounces) uncooked fusilli or
      spaghetti, hot cooked and drained
  2 tablespoons chopped parsley (optional)

Cook and stir mushrooms, peppers, onions, garlic, shallots, basil, oregano and red pepper in hot oil in large skillet until lightly browned. Add tomatoes with juice; bring to a boil. Reduce heat to low; simmer 20 minutes. Season to taste with salt and pepper. Place fusilli on plates. Spoon sauce over fusilli. Garnish with parsley.

he scallop has two shells like oysters and clams, but unlike them it swims in the water and moves along the ocean floor. A large muscle, sometimes called the eye, controls the movements of the shell. It is this muscle that opens and closes the shell and is the only part of the scallop that is usually eaten in North America.

Scallops with Vermicelli

♦ Maria Hannis from Plainfield, New Jersey was a finalist in the "Fishing for Compliments Recipe Contest" sponsored by the New Jersey Department of Agriculture.

Makes 4 servings

- 1 pound bay scallops
- 2 tablespoons fresh lemon juice
- 2 tablespoons chopped parsley
- 1 onion, chopped
- 1 clove garlic, minced
- 2 tablespoons olive oil
- 2 tablespoons butter, divided
- 1½ cups canned Italian tomatoes, undrained and cut up
- 2 tablespoons chopped fresh basil *or*
  ½ teaspoon dried basil, crushed
- ¼ teaspoon dried oregano leaves, crushed
- ¼ teaspoon dried thyme leaves, crushed
- 2 tablespoons heavy cream
  Dash ground nutmeg
- 12 ounces uncooked vermicelli, hot cooked and drained

Rinse scallops. Combine scallops, lemon juice and parsley in glass dish. Cover; marinate in refrigerator while preparing sauce.

Cook and stir onion and garlic in oil and 1 tablespoon of the butter in large skillet over medium-high heat until onion is tender. Add tomatoes with juice, basil, oregano and thyme. Reduce heat to low. Cover; simmer 30 minutes, stirring occasionally.

Drain scallops. Cook and stir scallops in remaining 1 tablespoon butter in another large skillet over medium heat until scallops are opaque, about 2 minutes. Add cream, nutmeg and tomato sauce.

Pour sauce over vermicelli in large bowl; toss gently to coat. Garnish as desired.

Buy fresh broccoli in bunches which are fresh-looking, ranging in color from dark green to purple-green. Bud clusters should be compact, showing no yellow color. Stalks and stems should also be green and fresh-looking. Avoid bunches with wilted, yellowed leaves.

Pasta and Broccoli

♦ Chef Frank Brogna from Boston, Massachusetts was a semifinalist in the "Use Your Noodle" contest sponsored by the National Pasta Association.

Makes 6 to 8 servings

- 1 bunch broccoli, steamed
- 1 clove garlic, finely chopped
- 2 tablespoons olive oil
- ¾ cup (3 ounces) shredded American or mozzarella cheese
- ½ cup grated Parmesan cheese
- ¼ cup butter
- ¼ cup chicken broth
- 3 tablespoons white wine
- 1 package (16 ounces) uncooked ziti macaroni, hot cooked and drained

Chop broccoli; set aside. Cook and stir garlic in hot oil in large skillet over medium-high heat until lightly browned. Add broccoli; cook and stir 3 to 4 minutes. Add American cheese, Parmesan cheese, butter, broth and wine; stir. Simmer until cheese melts.

Pour sauce over ziti in large bowl; toss gently to coat. Garnish as desired.

Penne with Artichokes

♦ Chef Angelo Nicelli from Chicago, Illinois was a prize winner in the "Use Your Noodle" contest sponsored by the National Pasta Association.

Makes 4 to 6 servings

  1 package (10 ounces) frozen artichokes
1¼ cups water
  2 tablespoons lemon juice
  5 cloves garlic, minced
  2 tablespoons olive oil, divided
  2 ounces sun-dried tomatoes, drained
  2 small dried hot red peppers, crushed
  2 tablespoons chopped parsley
  ¼ teaspoon salt
  ¼ teaspoon pepper
  ¾ cup fresh bread crumbs
  1 tablespoon chopped garlic
 12 ounces uncooked penne, hot cooked and
     drained
  1 tablespoon grated Romano cheese

Cook artichokes in water and lemon juice in medium saucepan over medium heat until tender. Cool artichokes, then cut into quarters. Reserve artichoke liquid.

Cook and stir the 5 whole cloves garlic in 1½ tablespoons oil in large skillet over medium-high heat until golden. Reduce heat to low. Add artichokes and tomatoes; simmer 1 minute. Stir in artichoke liquid, red peppers, parsley, salt and pepper. Simmer 5 minutes.

Meanwhile, cook and stir bread crumbs and 1 tablespoon chopped garlic in remaining ½ tablespoon oil. Pour artichoke sauce over penne in large bowl; toss gently to coat. Sprinkle with bread crumb mixture and cheese.

*P*umpkin has recently joined the ranks of fashionable foods. Suddenly we are seeing pumpkin ravioli, cheesecakes and relishes. When using fresh pumpkin, remember to save the seeds—they're tasty and nutritious, can be eaten raw or toasted and are a great addition to many dishes. Store them in the refrigerator in an airtight container.

Pumpkin Pasta Piccata

♦ Roxanne Chan from Albany, California was a prize winner in the Pumpkin Recipe Contest sponsored by Sterling Cookbooks.

Makes 8 servings

   4 cups half-and-half
   ½ cup margarine
   3 cups shredded peeled pumpkin
   2 green onions, finely chopped
   ½ cup chopped parsley
   ¼ cup chopped fresh dill
   2 tablespoons drained capers
   1 tablespoon grated lemon peel
   2 teaspoons Dijon mustard
   ¼ teaspoon pepper
   1 package (16 ounces) uncooked spinach
      fettuccine, hot cooked and drained
   Lemon slices (optional)
   Fresh dill sprigs (optional)

Heat half-and-half and margarine in medium saucepan over low heat until reduced to half, about 30 minutes. Add pumpkin, onions, parsley, chopped dill, capers, lemon peel, mustard and pepper. Simmer 5 minutes more, stirring constantly. Pour over fettuccine in large bowl; toss gently to coat. Garnish with lemon slices and dill sprigs.

Crabmeat obtained from the hard-shell crab is one of life's great luxuries. Conveniently available in cans, it will keep in the refrigerator for a few days after it is opened.

Crabmeat with Herbs and Pasta

♦ Yolanda Hansen from Paramus, New Jersey was a finalist in the "Fishing for Compliments Recipe Contest" sponsored by the New Jersey Department of Agriculture and Ronzoni Pasta.

Makes 4 servings

  1 small onion, minced
  1 carrot, shredded
  1 clove garlic, minced
  ⅓ cup olive oil
  3 tablespoons butter or margarine
  6 ounces flaked crabmeat
  ¼ cup chopped fresh basil *or* 1 teaspoon dried
       basil leaves, crushed
  2 tablespoons chopped parsley
  1 tablespoon lemon juice
  ½ cup chopped pine nuts (optional)
  ½ teaspoon salt
  ½ package (8 ounces) Ronzoni® Vermicelli, hot
       cooked and drained

Cook and stir onion, carrot and garlic in hot oil and butter in large skillet over medium-high heat until vegetables are tender, but not brown.
Reduce heat to medium. Stir in crabmeat, basil, parsley and lemon juice. Cook 4 minutes, stirring constantly. Stir in pine nuts and salt. Pour sauce over vermicelli in large bowl; toss gently to coat. Garnish as desired.

Pasta should be cooked at a fast boil. This method circulates the pasta so that it cooks more evenly.

Spinach Pesto

♦ Penny Lockhart was the third place winner in the Great Garlic Recipe Contest, sponsored by the Fresh Garlic Association and the Gilroy Garlic Festival, Gilroy, California.

Makes 2 cups sauce

- 1 bunch fresh spinach, washed, dried and chopped
- 1 cup fresh parsley leaves, stems removed
- ⅔ cup grated Parmesan cheese
- ½ cup walnut pieces
- 6 cloves fresh garlic, crushed
- 4 flat anchovy filets
- 1 tablespoon dried tarragon leaves, crushed
- 1 teaspoon dried basil leaves, crushed
- 1 teaspoon salt
- ½ teaspoon pepper
- ¼ teaspoon anise or fennel seed
- 1 cup olive oil
  Hot cooked spaghetti, pasta twists or shells
  Mixed salad (optional)

Place all ingredients except oil and pasta in covered food processor. Process until mixture is smooth. With motor running, add oil in thin stream. Adjust seasonings, if desired. Pour desired amount over pasta; toss gently to coat. Serve with mixed salad. Garnish as desired.

Note: Sauce will keep about 1 week in a covered container in the refrigerator.

*W*rap fresh ginger in a plastic bag and store in the refrigerator crisper for up to 2 weeks. To use fresh ginger, rinse and scrub outer skin before peeling with a sharp knife or vegetable peeler.

An Early Spring Pasta

◆ Chef Gregory Funk from Philadelphia, Pennsylvania was a semifinalist in the "Use Your Noodle" contest sponsored by the National Pasta Association.

Makes 4 to 6 servings

      1 cup Oriental Dressing (recipe follows)
      8 ounces cooked turkey breast, cut into
            julienne strips
      4 ounces carrots, cut into julienne strips
      4 ounces asparagus, diagonally sliced into
            1-inch pieces
      4 ounces spinach, chopped
    12 ounces uncooked linguine, hot cooked and
            drained

Heat Oriental Dressing in large saucepan over high heat to a boil. Add turkey, carrots, asparagus and spinach; reduce heat to medium. Cook 2 to 3 minutes. Pour sauce over linguine in large bowl; toss gently to coat.

Oriental Dressing

      1 large onion, sliced
      1 cup water
    ¼ cup *each* soy sauce and rice vinegar
      1 tablespoon *each* garlic and ginger root,
            minced
      1 tablespoon *each* sesame oil and lemon juice
    1½ teaspoons *each* sugar and pepper
    1½ teaspoons hot pepper sauce
      2 tablespoons cornstarch
    ¼ cup water

Spread onion on large baking pan. Heat in preheated 400°F. oven until edges are dark brown, about 15 minutes. Puree onion in covered food processor. Place onion and remaining ingredients except cornstarch and ¼ cup water in medium saucepan. Bring to a boil. Combine cornstarch and ¼ cup water in cup until smooth. Gradually stir into dressing mixture. Heat until mixture boils, stirring constantly. Reduce heat to low; simmer 2 to 3 minutes.

PASTA POTPOURRI

The word orzo actually means barley, even though the shape of this pasta looks more like rice. It is available in the pasta sections of large supermarkets.

Quick Beef Soup

♦ Aloiuse Michlitsch from Flasher, North Dakota was a prize winner in the North Dakota Beef Cook-Off sponsored by the North Dakota CattleWomen and the North Dakota Beef Commission.

Makes 6 servings

1½ pounds lean ground beef
  1 cup chopped onion
  2 cloves garlic, finely chopped
  1 can (28 ounces) tomatoes, undrained
  6 cups water
  6 beef bouillon cubes
  ¼ teaspoon pepper
  ½ cup uncooked orzo
1½ cups frozen peas, carrots and corn vegetable
     blend
    French bread (optional)

Cook beef, onion and garlic in large saucepan over medium-high heat until beef is brown, stirring to separate meat; drain fat.

Puree tomatoes with juice in covered blender or food processor. Add tomatoes, water, bouillon cubes and pepper to meat mixture. Bring to a boil; reduce heat to low. Simmer, uncovered, 20 minutes. Add orzo and vegetables. Simmer 15 minutes more. Serve with French bread.

Wisconsin Swiss Linguine Tart

♦ Michael Hove was a winner in the Supermarket Chef's Showcase sponsored by the Wisconsin Milk Marketing Board.

Makes 8 servings

½ cup butter, divided
2 cloves garlic, minced
30 thin French bread slices
3 tablespoons all-purpose flour
1 teaspoon salt
¼ teaspoon white pepper
Dash ground nutmeg
2½ cups milk
¼ cup grated Wisconsin Parmesan cheese
2 eggs, beaten
8 ounces fresh linguine, cooked and drained
2 cups (8 ounces) shredded Wisconsin Swiss cheese, divided
⅓ cup sliced green onions
2 tablespoons minced fresh basil *or* 1 teaspoon dried basil leaves, crushed
2 plum tomatoes, each cut lengthwise into eights

Melt ¼ cup butter in small saucepan over medium heat. Add garlic; cook 1 minute. Brush 10-inch pie plate with butter mixture. Line bottom and side of pie plate with bread, allowing up to 1-inch overhang. Brush bread with remaining butter mixture. Bake in preheated 400°F. oven 5 minutes or until lightly browned.

Melt remaining ¼ cup butter in medium saucepan over low heat. Stir in flour and seasonings. Gradually stir in milk; cook, stirring constantly, until thickened. Add Parmesan cheese. Stir some of the sauce into eggs; stir back into sauce. Set aside. Combine linguine, 1¼ cups of the Swiss cheese, onions and basil in large bowl. Pour sauce over linguine mixture; toss to coat. Pour into crust. Arrange tomatoes on top; sprinkle with remaining ¾ cup Swiss cheese. Bake in preheated 350°F. oven 25 minutes or until warm; let stand 5 minutes. Garnish as desired.

Most pastas are prepared with wheat flours or other cereal grains and water. If an egg is added to this mix, the product is then called a noodle.

Shaker Chicken and Noodle Soup

♦ Lorraine Bourgois from Bismarck, North Dakota was a runner-up in the Savory Soups Pasta Contest sponsored by the North Dakota Wheat Commission.

Makes 15 servings

> 13 cups chicken broth, divided
> ¼ cup dry vermouth
> ¼ cup butter or margarine
> 1 cup heavy cream
> 1 package (12 ounces) frozen or dry egg noodles
> 1½ cups water
> ¾ cup all-purpose flour
> 2 cups diced cooked chicken
> Salt and pepper to taste
> ¼ cup finely chopped parsley (optional)

Combine 1 cup broth, vermouth and butter in small saucepan. Bring to a boil and cook until liquid is reduced to ¼ cup and has a syrupy consistency. Stir in cream; set aside.

Bring remaining broth to a boil in Dutch oven. Add noodles and cook until just tender. Combine water and flour in medium bowl until smooth. Stir into broth mixture. Boil for 2 minutes, stirring constantly. Stir in reserved cream mixture; add chicken. Season to taste with salt and pepper. Heat just to serving temperature. Do not boil. Sprinkle with parsley. Garnish as desired.

Note: This soup freezes well.

Stuffed Seafood Shells

♦ Clarice Moberg from Redstone, Montana was the first place winner in the Appetizing Appetizers Pasta Contest sponsored by the North Dakota Wheat Commission.

Makes 8 appetizer servings

    1 can (6½ ounces) tuna, drained and flaked
    1 can (4½ ounces) medium shrimp, drained
    ½ cup pearl onions, cooked and sliced
    ½ cup chopped sweet pickles
    ½ cup sliced pimiento-stuffed olives
    1 bottle (12 ounces) chili sauce
    2 tablespoons bottled horseradish sauce
    ½ teaspoon Worcestershire sauce
      Hot pepper sauce to taste
   16 jumbo pasta shells, cooked, rinsed and
      drained
      Bibb lettuce leaves

Combine tuna, shrimp, onions, pickles and olives in large bowl. Combine chili sauce, horseradish sauce, Worcestershire and hot pepper sauce to taste in small bowl; blend well. Pour over seafood mixture; mix gently. Cover and refrigerate at least 30 minutes. Fill cooked shells with seafood mixture. (Shells may be covered and refrigerated several hours.) Serve over lettuce. Garnish as desired.

Peeling Garlic Cloves

To peel whole garlic cloves, trim off the ends and drop cloves into boiling water for 5 to 10 seconds. Immediately plunge into cold water, then drain. The peels should slip right off. If the cloves are to be minced, trim off the ends and crush with the bottom of a heavy saucepan or the flat side of a large knife. The peels can then be easily removed. For information on peeling cloves by microwave oven method, see page 18.

Spinach-Garlic Pasta with Garlic-Onion Sauce

♦ Ira Jacobson from Oakland, California was third place winner in the Great Garlic Recipe Contest, sponsored by the Fresh Garlic Association in association with the Gilroy Garlic Festival, Gilroy, California.

Makes 2 to 4 servings

SPINACH-GARLIC PASTA
1½ cups all-purpose flour, divided
  2 eggs *plus* 4 yolks
  1 tablespoon olive oil
  ½ pound fresh spinach, blanched, squeezed
     dry and finely chopped
  6 large cloves fresh garlic, crushed and finely
     chopped
  ½ teaspoon salt

GARLIC-ONION SAUCE
  ½ cup butter
  1 tablespoon olive oil
  1 pound Vidalia or other sweet onions, sliced
  ⅓ cup chopped fresh garlic (about 12 large
     cloves)
  1 tablespoon honey (optional)
  ¼ cup Marsala wine
    Grated Parmesan cheese (optional)

For pasta, place 1 cup flour in large bowl. Make well in center; place eggs, yolks and olive oil in well. Add spinach, garlic and salt. Mix, working in more flour as needed. Knead until dough is smooth. Cover with plastic wrap. Let rest 15 to 30 minutes. Roll dough to desired thickness with pasta machine. Cut into desired width. Cook in boiling water about 2 minutes; drain.

For sauce, heat butter and oil in large skillet over medium heat. Add onions and garlic; cover and cook until soft. Add honey; reduce heat to low. Cook, uncovered, 30 minutes, stirring occasionally. Add wine; cook 5 to 10 minutes more. Pour sauce over pasta; toss gently to coat. Serve with cheese. Garnish as desired.

It is from the durum and other hard wheats that pasta receives its yellow amber color, nutty flavor and ability to retain its shape and firmness when cooked. The United States produces 15% of the world's durum wheat. Of that amount, North Dakota produces about 75%. Our durum is prized by other pasta loving countries, so much so, that over 60 million bushels are exported each year to countries, such as Italy and France.

Zucchini-Tomato-Noodle Soup

♦ Eleanor Magrum from Braddock, North Dakota was a third place winner in the Savory Soups Pasta Contest sponsored by the North Dakota Wheat Commission.

Makes 8 servings

 10 cups cubed zucchini
 ¾ cup water
  4 cups chopped onion
 ½ cup butter
  8 cups quartered tomatoes
  4 chicken bouillon cubes
  3 cloves garlic, chopped
  1 teaspoon Beau Monde seasoning
  1 teaspoon salt
  1 teaspoon pepper
  4 cups uncooked 100% durum noodles, hot
     cooked and drained
    Garlic bread (optional)

Combine zucchini and water in Dutch oven. Cook over medium heat until partially done. Cook and stir onion in hot butter in small skillet over medium heat until tender. Add onion mixture, tomatoes, bouillon cubes, garlic, seasoning, salt and pepper to zucchini mixture. Simmer until tender. Add noodles; heat through. Serve with garlic bread.

Almond Crunch Macaroni Custard

♦ Linda Jung from Norwich, North Dakota was first place winner in the Delicious Desserts Pasta Contest sponsored by the North Dakota Wheat Commission.

Makes 9 servings

CUSTARD
   2 eggs
   1 cup milk
   ½ cup packed brown sugar
   ¼ cup all-purpose flour
   ¼ cup butter, softened
   1½ teaspoons almond extract
   ½ cup uncooked ring macaroni, cooked and
       drained

ALMOND TOPPING
   ½ cup slivered almonds
   ⅓ cup packed brown sugar
   2 tablespoons butter, softened
   1 tablespoon milk

For custard, combine all custard ingredients except macaroni in covered blender. Blend on medium speed 2 minutes. Fold macaroni into milk mixture in large bowl. Spoon into greased and floured 8-inch square pan. Bake in preheated 350°F. oven 40 to 45 minutes or until set.

For almond topping, mix all topping ingredients in small bowl. Spread over custard. Broil 2 to 3 minutes or until topping is bubbly and golden brown. Garnish as desired.

Creamy Shell Soup

♦ Grace Faul from McClusky, North Dakota was first place winner in the Savory Soups Pasta Contest sponsored by the North Dakota Wheat Commission.

Makes 8 servings

  4 cups water
  3 to 4 chicken pieces
  1 cup diced onions
  ¼ cup chopped celery
  ¼ cup minced parsley *or* 1 tablespoon dried
      parsley flakes
  1 bay leaf
  1 teaspoon salt
  ¼ teaspoon white pepper
  2 medium potatoes, diced
  4 to 5 green onions, chopped
  3 chicken bouillon cubes
  ½ teaspoon seasoned salt
  ½ teaspoon poultry seasoning
  4 cups milk
  2 cups medium shell macaroni, cooked and
      drained
  ¼ cup butter or margarine
  ¼ cup all-purpose flour
      Ground nutmeg
      Chopped fresh parsley

Simmer water, chicken, diced onions, celery, minced parsley, bay leaf, salt and pepper in Dutch oven until chicken is tender. Remove bay leaf; discard. Remove chicken; cool. Skin and debone; set aside.

Add potatoes, green onions, bouillon cubes, seasoned salt and poultry seasoning to broth. Simmer 15 minutes. Add milk, macaroni and chicken; return to simmer.

Melt butter over medium heat. Add flour, stirring constantly, until mixture begins to brown. Add to soup; blend well. Let soup stand 20 minutes to blend flavors. Season to taste. Garnish with nutmeg and chopped parsley.

INDEX

Almond Crunch Macaroni Custard, 92
Almond Topping, 92
An Early Spring Pasta, 78
Appetizers
    Fettuccine with Duckling and Roasted Red Peppers, 56
    Fresh Tomato Pasta Andrew, 58
    Stuffed Seafood Shells, 86
Apple Lasagna, 54

Basil Vinaigrette Dressing, 10
Beef Oriental, 30

Cheese and Eggs
    Fresh Tomato Pasta Andrew, 58
    Rigatoni with Four Cheeses, 42
    Saucy Mediterranean Frittata, 24
    Wisconsin Swiss Linguine Tart, 82
Cheesy Chicken Roll-Ups, 38
Chicken Salad Deluxe, 12
Crabmeat with Herbs and Pasta, 74
Creamy Shell Soup, 94

Desserts
    Almond Crunch Macaroni Custard, 92
    Apple Lasagna, 54
Dressings and Sauces
    Basil Vinaigrette Dressing, 10
    Garlic-Onion Sauce, 88
    Oriental Dressing, 78
    Spinach Pesto, 76

Fettuccine with Duckling and Roasted Red Peppers, 56
Fresh Seafood and Linguine Salad, 16
Fresh Tomato Pasta Andrew, 58
Fusilli Pizziaola, 64

Garlic cloves, peeling, 18, 88
Garlic-Onion Sauce, 88

Lasagna Supreme, 48
Lazy Lasagna, 44
Luscious Vegetarian Lasagna, 50

Meat
    Beef Oriental, 30
    Lasagna Supreme, 48
    Lazy Lasagna, 44
    Polish Reuben Casserole, 40
    Quick Beef Soup, 80
    Spaghetti Rolls, 26
    Spetzque, 52
    String Pie, 36
    Sunday Super Stuffed Shells, 32
    Tacos in Pasta Shells, 22

Oriental Dressing, 78

Pasta and Broccoli, 68
Pasta Delight, 62
Pasta, homemade: Spinach-Garlic Pasta with Garlic-Onion Sauce, 88
Pasta Salad in Artichoke Cups, 10
Penne with Artichokes, 70
Polish Reuben Casserole, 40

Poultry
    An Early Spring Pasta, 78
    Cheesy Chicken Roll-Ups, 38
    Chicken Salad Deluxe, 12
    Creamy Shell Soup, 94
    Fettuccine with Duckling and Roasted Red Peppers, 56
    Shaker Chicken and Noodle Soup, 84
    Sweet Garlic with Chicken Pasta, 18
    Thai Chicken Fettuccine Salad, 6
Pumpkin Pasta Piccata, 72

Quick Beef Soup, 80

Rainbow Pasta Salad, 8
Rigatoni with Four Cheeses, 42
Rotini Salad, 14

Saucy Mediterranean Frittata, 24
Scallops with Vermicelli, 66
Seafood
    Crabmeat with Herbs and Pasta, 74
    Fresh Seafood and Linguine Salad, 16
    Rainbow Pasta Salad, 8
    Scallops with Vermicelli, 66
    Seafood Lasagne, 46
    Seafood Pea-Ista Salad, 4
    Shrimp in Angel Hair Pasta Casserole, 28
    Shrimp Noodle Supreme, 34
    Stuffed Seafood Shells, 86
    Vegetable Seafood Pasta, 60
Shaker Chicken and Noodle Soup, 84
Shrimp in Angel Hair Pasta Casserole, 28
Shrimp Noodle Supreme, 34
Soups
    Creamy Shell Soup, 94
    Quick Beef Soup, 80
    Shaker Chicken and Noodle Soup, 84
    Zucchini-Tomato-Noodle Soup, 90
Spaghetti Rolls, 26
Spetzque, 52
Spinach-Garlic Pasta with Garlic-Onion Sauce, 88
Spinach Pesto, 76
Spinach Stuffed Manicotti, 20
Squid, cleaning, 16
String Pie, 36
Stuffed Seafood Shells, 86
Sunday Super Stuffed Shells, 32
Sweet Garlic with Chicken Pasta, 18

Tacos in Pasta Shells, 22
Thai Chicken Fettuccine Salad, 6

Vegetables
    Fresh Tomato Pasta Andrew, 58
    Fusilli Pizziaola, 64
    Garlic-Onion Sauce, 88
    Luscious Vegetarian Lasagna, 50
    Pasta and Broccoli, 68
    Pasta Delight, 62
    Pasta Salad in Artichoke Cups, 10
    Penne with Artichokes, 70
    Pumpkin Pasta Piccata, 72
    Rotini Salad, 14
    Spinach Pesto, 76
    Spinach Stuffed Manicotti, 20
    Zucchini-Tomato-Noodle Soup, 90
Vegetable Seafood Pasta, 60

Wisconsin Swiss Linguine Tart, 82

Zucchini-Tomato-Noodle Soup, 90